American Lives

Benjamin Banneker

Rick Burke

Heinemann Library
Chicago, Illinois

© 2003 Heinemann Library
a division of Reed Elsevier Inc.
Chicago, Illinois

Customer Service 888-454-2279

Visit our website at www.heinemannlibrary.com

Created by the publishing team
at Heinemann Library

Designed by Sarah Figlio
Photo Research by Dawn Friedman
Printed and Bound in the United States by
Lake Book Manufacturing, Inc.

07 06 05 04 03
10 9 8 7 6 5 4 3 2 1

Library of Congress Cataloging-in-Publication Data
Burke, Rick, 1957-
  Benjamin Banneker / Rick Burke.
    v. cm. — (American lives)
  Includes bibliographical references and index.
  Contents: A hunger for knowledge — Molly —
Benjamin's family history — Young Benjamin —
The wooden clock — Life goes on — The Ellicott
family — Astronomy — Roads to other places —
Washington, D.C. — Almanacs — A letter to
Thomas Jefferson — Benjamin's final years.
    ISBN 1-4034-0725-8 (lib. bdg. : hardcover) —
ISBN 1-4034-3100-0 (pbk.)
  1. Banneker, Benjamin, 1731-1806—Juvenile
literature. 2. Astronomers—United States—
Biography—Juvenile literature. 3. African
American scientists—Biography—Juvenile literature.
[1. Banneker, Benjamin, 1731-1806. 2. Astronomers.
3. Scientists. 4. African
Americans—Biography.] I. Title.
  QB36.B22B87 2003
  520'.92—dc21
                              2002154413

Acknowledgments
The author and publishers are grateful to the
following for permission to reproduce copyright
material: Title page, p. 5 Stock Montage, Inc.; p. 4
portrait by Hughie Lee Smith/Collection of the
Banneker-Douglass Museum, Annapolis, MD; p. 6
Historical Picture Archive/Corbis; pp. 7, 15 North
Wind Picture Archives; pp. 8, 11, 18, 20, 25, 27
Bettmann/Corbis; pp. 9, 24 Hulton Archive/Getty
Images; p. 12 Collection of the Spruance Library of
the Bucks County Historical Society, PA; p. 13
History of Technology Division, National Museum
of American History, Smithsonian Institution; p. 14
Victoria & Albert Museum, London/Art Resource,
NY; pp. 16, 17, 19 Maryland Historical Society;
p. 21 Smithsonian Institution Libraries; p. 22
Library of Congress; p. 23 Schomburg Center for
Research in Black Culture/New York Public
Library; p. 26 Thomas Jefferson Papers Series 1,
General Correspondence 1651-1827, Library of
Congress; p. 28 Maryland Historical Trust; p. 29
1980© .15¢ Benjamin Banneker - Scott #1804,
United States Postal Service. Displayed with
permission. All rights reserved. Written
authorization from the Postal Service is
required to use, reproduce, post, transmit,
distribute, or publicly display these images.

Cover photograph: Stock Montage, Inc.

Special thanks to Patrick Halladay for his help in
the preparation of this book.

Every effort has been made to contact copyright
holders of any material reproduced in this book.
Any omissions will be rectified in subsequent
printings if notice is given to the publisher.

Some words are shown in bold, **like this.** You can
find out what they mean by looking in the glossary.

For more information on the image of Benjamin Banneker
that appears on the cover of this book, turn to page 5.

Contents

A Hunger for Knowledge

Benjamin Banneker was an interesting man who lived in difficult times. He was the son and grandson of **slaves.** He was born in the American **colonies** of Great Britain and saw the beginning of a new nation. He learned how to read when few people in the colonies could. He owned land and made a good living as a farmer. But what made Benjamin famous was his hunger for knowledge and his ability to teach himself what he wanted to learn.

African-American artist Hughie Lee-Smith painted this picture of Banneker.

Music Man

Benjamin played the violin and flute, which he had taught himself to play as a young man.

Benjamin was born in the colony of Maryland in 1731. He lived most of his life there. He did not go to school very long. But he spent his free time learning everything he could about the things that interested him. He learned by reading. He was a scientist, an inventor, a farmer, a **surveyor,** an author, and a musician. Through his knowledge, skills, and deeds, he showed the people of the young United States that people of all races were equally important.

This image of Benjamin Banneker was printed using a design that was cut in a piece of wood.

Molly

Benjamin's story begins with his grandmother, Molly Walsh. Molly was a white **servant** in Great Britain. One day, after milking a cow, she tripped over the bucket and spilled the milk. The owner of the farm didn't

This painting from 1808 shows how people used to carry buckets of milk.

believe that it was an accident. He said Molly had stolen the milk. In those times, Molly could have been hanged for stealing.

Molly had to go to court. The judge asked Molly if she knew how to read. Since she could read, Molly was sent to the American **colonies** as an **indentured servant** in 1698.

The Life of Benjamin Banneker

1731	1753	1771	1789
Born on November 9 near Baltimore, Maryland.	*Built a wooden clock at age 22.*	*Ellicott family moves near Benjamin's farm.*	*Made his first **ephemeris**.*

An indentured servant was forced to work for whomever paid for his or her boat ticket to the colonies. Molly had to work for a farmer in Maryland for seven years. When her seven years were up, Molly wanted her own farm. She worked hard for other farmers for money, and she was able to buy a small place.

The ship that Molly traveled to the colonies on probably looked a lot like this one. The front of the ship is shown in the painting above.

The land was along the Patapsco River, near Baltimore, Maryland. She worked even harder and bought two male **slaves** who were forced to come to the colonies from Africa. The slaves helped her do heavy work on the farm.

1791	**1791**	**1791**	**1806**
Helped **survey** *land to build Washington, D.C.*	*First* **almanac** **published.**	*Wrote a letter to Thomas Jefferson.*	*Died on October 25 in Maryland.*

Benjamin's Family History

One of Molly's **slaves** did not like working in the fields. He said he had been a prince in Africa. A prince was the son of a king who ruled a village or tribe. His said his name was Banna Ka.

After a few years, Molly gave both slaves their freedom. She fell in love with Banna Ka. Molly and Banna Ka

After slaves were forced off the ships, they were sold to the people who offered to pay the most.

married, even though it was against the law for a white woman to marry a slave. If they had been caught, they would have been killed. Over the years, the name Banna Ka became the family name of Banneker. Molly and Banna Ka had four children.

Banna Ka's Death

One day when Banna Ka was hunting, a bolt of lightning hit a tree and split it in half. As it crashed to the ground, part of the tree fell on Banna Ka and killed him.

When Molly and Banna Ka's daughter Mary was sixteen, she bought a slave named Robert to work on the farm. Just like her mother, Mary set her slave free, and just like her mother, she fell in love with the person she freed. Mary and Robert got married. The couple lived with Molly and helped her farm the land.

This notice of slaves for sale in Boston, Massachusetts, is from about 1700.

Young Benjamin

When they saved enough money, Mary and Robert bought their own farm near Molly's land. Mary and Robert had their first child in 1731. They named him Benjamin. The couple also had three daughters. Molly taught Benjamin how to read from the only book she owned, the Bible. Benjamin liked to read and write, but he really liked solving math problems.

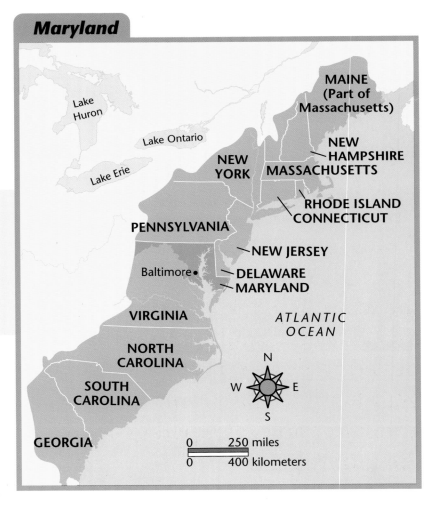

Maryland

Maryland, the **colony** where the Bannekers lived, is shown in dark green on this map.

This artwork shows what a tobacco farm in the colony of Virginia looked like in 1714.

The Bannekers grew tobacco on their farm. It was hard work. Benjamin helped his parents do whatever needed to be done on the farm. He helped chop down trees so that tobacco plants could be grown. He pulled weeds so the tobacco plants could get plenty of water and sunlight. He fed the animals, and he helped grow vegetables in the family garden.

The Wooden Clock

Benjamin learned everything Molly had to teach him. Then, Molly convinced Benjamin's parents to send Benjamin to a school near the farm. The school taught both white children and African-American children. Schools that taught African-Americans were rare in the **colonies.**

Benjamin went to the school during the winter, when his parents didn't need his help on the farm. Benjamin really liked to learn, especially about numbers and how they worked with each other. He liked to make his own math puzzles and riddles for others to solve.

In Benjamin's time, many schoolhouses were shaped like the one in this photo. It was built in the 1700s in Pennsylvania.

When Benjamin was 22, he did something amazing. He built a clock that was made mostly of wood. There wasn't much of a need for watches or clocks where Benjamin lived. People started work when the sun came up and stopped when it got dark. But Benjamin was fascinated by clocks. He wanted to try to build one.

Benjamin's clock was the first built in America that rang hourly. It probably looked like the clock above.

Benjamin had met a traveling salesperson named Josef Levi. He loaned Benjamin a pocket watch. Benjamin took it apart to see how it worked. Benjamin then made his own clock. He carved the gears from wood and made the clock work.

Life Goes On

Benjamin's clock worked! Benjamin added a bell so that the clock would ring every hour. Neighbors came from miles away to see Benjamin's clock. For the next 50 years, the clock kept the right time.

Benjamin figured out how the gears in watches worked. Later in life, he started a business that fixed watches.

What Benjamin did was special. His clock was one of the first clocks to be built in the **colonies.** But people who trained to be clockmakers made the other clocks. Benjamin was able to build his clock by using mathematics. He simply changed the size of the gears he saw in a borrowed pocket watch.

The first book Benjamin bought was a Bible like the one shown in the photo.

Six years after he built the clock, Benjamin's father, Robert, died. His three sisters married, and they moved away. Molly had also died. Benjamin and his mother, Mary, had to do all the work on the farm by themselves.

Benjamin never married, maybe because he was shy. It was easier for him to talk to other people about ideas and science than it was to talk about himself and his feelings. Benjamin bought his first book in 1763 when he was 32. He bought a Bible from a neighbor. He spent his quiet evenings reading his new book.

The Ellicott Family

Benjamin's life began to change when the Ellicott family moved near Benjamin's farm in 1771. The five Ellicott brothers came to Maryland from Pennsylvania to build a **mill.**

Maryland

PENNSYLVANIA

MARYLAND

Patapsco River

Baltimore

Ellicott Mill

Washington, D.C.

N
W   E
S

0   60 miles
0   100 kilometers

This map shows how close the Ellicotts' mill was to Baltimore.

The mill was located on the Patapsco River, very close to Benjamin's farm. At the mill, a large paddle wheel would dip down into the river and power big, heavy stones that crushed grain. This made flour. The Ellicotts belonged to a religious group called the Society of Friends, or the Quakers.

This artwork shows the Ellicotts' mill in Maryland.

Quakers believe that everyone, whether they were black or white, should be treated with respect. Even though about half the families in the area owned at least one **slave,** the Ellicotts did not use slaves to work at their mill. They paid all their workers.

Benjamin lived about one mile (1.6 kilometers) away. He liked to wander over to where the mill was being built and talk to the Ellicott brothers. Benjamin and George Ellicott became good friends.

This a letter that Benjamin Banneker wrote to George Ellicott in 1789.

Astronomy

One of George's hobbies was astronomy. Astronomy is the study of planets and stars. A person who studies astronomy is an astronomer. George Ellicott sometimes invited Benjamin to look at the stars with him.

George became busier working at the **mill.** He no longer had time for astronomy. He packed up his astronomy books and **telescope** and brought them to Benjamin's house. He promised to come back to show Benjamin how to use the telescope.

This is the type of telescope that Benjamin might have used.

This is the journal in which Benjamin kept track of what he saw in the night sky.

Benjamin could not wait. He read all the books and began to look through the telescope right away. What he saw thrilled him. He would gaze at the stars all night. When the sun came up, he would put away the telescope and do all the work that needed to be done on the farm. In the afternoon, he would take a short nap.

Roads to Other Places

George Ellicott was also a **surveyor.** This was an important job. The country was growing and there was a need for roads to get people from one place to another. George measured the land with a tool called a **transit.** He had to find the best places to build roads. Workers would follow behind him and clear the land of trees and make it level.

Benjamin thought surveying was interesting. George loaned him some books and tools, and Benjamin taught himself how to survey.

This painting shows a crew of surveyors on January 12, 1730, planning how to lay out the city of Baltimore.

By 1789, Benjamin had become such a good astronomer that he wanted to make his own **ephemeris.** An ephemeris is a table or chart that shows where the stars and planets will be in the sky every night. Benjamin could predict where the stars would be in his ephemeris.

He sent the ephemeris away to be checked for errors. But by the time it was found to be correct, it was too late to print it in an **almanac.** The new year had already started.

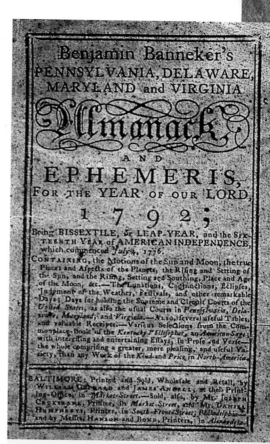

Benjamin Banneker's almanac and ephemeris from 1792 is shown above.

Ephemeris

An ephemeris was always printed in an almanac. Farmers used almanacs to know when to plant their crops, and sailors used ephemerides to help them sail their ships. Sailors could tell what direction they were sailing by where the stars were in the sky.

Washington, D.C.

When Benjamin was almost 60 years old, he took on a new challenge. In January 1791, United States President George Washington picked Major Andrew Ellicott IV to **survey** the land that would become the new capital of the United States, Washington, D.C.

Washington's cousin Andrew Ellicott directed the other surveyors.

Andrew wanted George Ellicott to help him with the job, but George was busy with other projects. George told Andrew that Benjamin was a skilled surveyor, and Benjamin was hired for the job.

The Nation's Capital

The first capital of the United States was New York City. Philadelphia was the second. It was then moved to Washington, D.C., because the city would be in the center of the new country. The states of Virginia and Maryland gave up land to make the city of Washington, D.C.

Major Pierre Charles L'Enfant was in charge of designing the city. But he left the job, returned to France, and took his designs of the city with him. It looked like months of work would be lost.

Benjamin saved the project. He had surveyed the same land as L'Enfant. He helped make new plans so that work could go on. President Washington, who was a surveyor when he was a young man, visited the area when the work was being done. Some

Benjamin is shown above going over the plans for Washington, D.C. The surveying was finished on January 1, 1793.

people who study history have said that Benjamin and Washington met and talked about surveying.

Almanacs

Benjamin left the **surveying** job in April 1791. He needed to plant the crops on his farm. He also wanted to try again to have his **ephemeris** printed in an **almanac.** By using math, Benjamin figured out when every sunrise, sunset, moonrise, and moonset would be for the next year. He also showed where the planets and stars would be in the sky.

BANNEKER's
ALMANACK,
AND
EPHEMERIS
FOR THE
YEAR OF OUR LORD 1793;
BEING
THE FIRST AFTER BISSEXTILE OR LEAP-YEAR:
CONTAINING
THE MOTIONS OF THE SUN AND MOON;
THE TRUE PLACES AND ASPECTS OF THE PLANETS;
THE RISING AND SETTING OF THE SUN;
RISING, SETTING, AND SOUTHING OF THE MOON;
THE LUNATIONS, CONJUNCTIONS, AND ECLIPSES;
AND
THE RISING, SETTING, AND SOUTHING OF THE PLANETS AND NOTED FIXED STARS.

PHILADELPHIA:
PRINTED AND SOLD BY JOSEPH CRUKSHANK, NO. 87, STREET

This is the first page of Banneker's almanac and ephemeris from 1793.

Moonrise and Moonset

Moonrise is the time when the moon first appears in the sky. Moonset is the time when the moon is no longer visible in the sky.

Phillis Wheatley

*Joseph Crukshank also printed the poems of Phillis Wheatley, a former **slave**.*

Almanacs were important. Besides an ephemeris, they contained articles, stories, and poems. If a family could read, they usually had two books in their house, a Bible and an almanac.

William Goddard, a printer in Baltimore, Maryland, **published** the ephemeris that Benjamin finished. Benjamin also had his ephemeris printed by Philadelphia printer Joseph Crukshank. Crukshank was an abolitionist. An abolitionist believed that **slaves** should be freed, and that black people were as skilled and smart as whites were.

Benjamin Bannaker's
PENNSYLVANIA, DELAWARE, MARYLAND, AND VIRGINIA
ALMANAC,
FOR THE
YEAR of our LORD 1795;
Being the Third after Leap-Year.

BANNAKER.

PHILADELPHIA:
Printed for WILLIAM GIBBONS, Cherry Street

On this 1795 almanac, Banneker's last name was spelled differently from the way people spell it today.

A Letter to Thomas Jefferson

Benjamin was a shy man. He didn't like to bring attention to himself, so writing a letter to a famous person was not easy for him. But Benjamin also knew that some people in the United States needed to change the way they thought.

This is Thomas Jefferson's reply to Banneker's letter.

African-American people had much to offer to the country. Benjamin wanted the people of the nation to know that African-Americans were just as smart and creative as white people were.

Jefferson the Scientist

Jefferson was a scientist, too, like Banneker. He loved to watch and record what happened in nature. Jefferson was elected the third president of the United States in 1800.

Benjamin wrote a letter to Thomas Jefferson, the **Secretary of State** for the United States, in August 1791. Jefferson was one of the smartest and most powerful men in the country.

Benjamin asked Jefferson to help him change the way the people of the United States thought about African-Americans. Jefferson wrote back saying that he wanted to help make that happen someday. Benjamin's letter to Jefferson and his **ephemeris** were printed in **almanacs** for the next few years.

Jefferson wrote the **Declaration of Independence,** part of which states that all men are created equal.

Benjamin's Final Years

In the last years of his life, Benjamin sold most of his land. He had made enough money by selling things he wrote. He didn't have to farm anymore. He spent his time keeping bees for the honey they made. And he spent many nights looking at the stars.

On October 25, 1806, Benjamin died after going for a walk. During his funeral, his cabin, which was miles away, suddenly caught fire. The fire burned everything in the cabin, including the wooden clock that Benjamin made. Nobody knows how the fire started.

Recently, scientists searched the site where Banneker's cabin used to be. They found things from his time, like nails, cups, and plates.

Benjamin Banneker

Black Heritage USA 15c

The United States Postal Service made this stamp available on February 15, 1980.

Benjamin showed the people of the United States that how smart a person was did not depend on the color of his or her skin. Benjamin is an example of what people can do when they try to be the best they can be. Benjamin taught himself as much as he could, and then he shared his knowledge with the rest of the world.

Glossary

almanac book that comes out each year that has a calendar and weather forecasts and lists facts about ocean tides, sunsets, and sunrises

colony group of people who moved to another land but who are still ruled by the country they moved from. People who live in a colony are called colonists.

Declaration of Independence document that said the United States was an independent nation. Independent means not under the control or rule of another person or government.

ephemeris table that shows where the stars and planets will be in the sky every night

indentured servant person who worked, usually for seven years, to pay off a debt

mill building where grain is ground into flour

publish to make books available for people to buy

Secretary of State person who is responsible for making sure the United States stays friendly with other countries around the world

servant attendant or helper

slave person who is owned by another person

surveyor person who measures and makes maps of land

telescope tool with lenses used to see objects that are far away

transit tool used in surveying to measure angles

More Books to Read

Blue, Rose. *Benjamin Banneker: Mathematician and Stargazer.* Brookfield, Conn.: Millwork Press, 2001.

Burke, Rick. *George Washington.* Chicago: Heinemann Library, 2002.

Burke, Rick. *Thomas Jefferson.* Chicago: Heinemann Library, 2002.

Hinman, Bonnie. *Benjamin Banneker: American Mathematician and Astronomer.* Broomall, Pa.: Chelsea House Publishers, 1999.

Pinkney, Andrea Davis. *Dear Benjamin Banneker.* New York: Harcourt Children's Books, 1998.

Places to Visit

Benjamin Banneker Historical Park and Museum
300 Oella Avenue
Catonsville, Maryland 21228
Visitor Information: (410) 887-1081

Banneker-Douglass Museum
84 Franklin Street
Annapolis, Maryland 21401
Visitor Information: (410) 216-6180

Index